ROUNDABOUTS
of
GREAT BRITAIN

ROUNDABOUTS
of
GREAT BRITAIN

KEVIN BERESFORD

INTRODUCTION

Our story begins in the run up to Christmas 2002 at my printing company B.B. Print Digital Limited, based in Redditch, Worcestershire.

Wondering what kind of calendar to give out to our clients and being totally bored with the usual array of Beckhams, Kylies and naked old ladies, we racked our brains and came up with the most unique calendar in history... "The Roundabouts of Redditch" – 12 stunning pictures of the very best traffic-islands Worcestershire had to offer. Redditch is a town most famous for needles and fish-hooks, it doesn't have a cinema but it does have three prisons and a 24-hour Tesco, and it also happens to be home to 41 splendid roundabouts.

We ran off ten copies on our recently-acquired digital press to try out on our clients, not realising that they would shake the world...

Responses ranged from hoots of derision to howls of laughter to a little bit of head-scratching. Other people actually found the subject matter very interesting. They would comment on the different aspects of one particular traffic-island and the individuality of another, all the while keeping a straight face. Another print-run was commissioned, this time 100 copies – all of which were immediately gobbled up by delighted customers. We knew we were on to a winner!

Then Jason Holmes, our production manager, sent a copy of the calendar to the comedian Graham Norton, who featured it on his TV show "So Graham Norton". As one of his guests was the Greek singer Nana Mouskouri, he presented her with a calendar of picturesque Hellenic islands, then showed her how the islands of Redditch compare. How pleasing that a town as modest as Redditch was finally proving to the world that it has something to offer.

Redditch Council called us to the town hall. They were worried about us denigrating the image of the town. A few years previously, Redditch had been awarded the unwanted accolade of "most boring postcard in Britain" – a picture of the town's bus station. Unsurprisingly they felt rather uneasy about all the publicity we had been receiving... Before leaving the town hall, I'd sold them around 200 copies.

Jason was tearing his hair out. We were doing more television interviews than our regular printing orders. It became a common occurrence for me to fit in an interview for Radio Norway. My mailbag was growing on a daily basis with letters from people of all walks of life enthusing over their favourite roundabouts. Stranger still, I was growing equally as enthusiastic, agreeing or disagreeing over the merits of countless roundabouts the length and breadth of Britain.

Ever since, my poor wife Linda has had to put up with me pulling the car over whenever an interesting roundabout appears before us. She patiently endures the spectacle of her husband scampering all over the island and giving it a thorough inspection, often making us late for appointments.

Islands have always played a large part in my life. I am a resident of the British Isles; I worked on the north island of New Zealand printing bank notes; I also lived for four years on the island of Tenerife selling timeshares. In fact, it was there on that island that I met Linda. Perhaps it was fate... Similarly with traffic-islands, interest became infatuation. Now I'm in full-blown love with roundabouts.

➡️ A great combination of kerbstone, chevron brickwork and grass topped with four directional signs and an international-looking backdrop. It almost has a golf-tee look to it.

➡️ No this roundabout was not discovered in China. The pagoda-style buildings are in fact Birmingham's Wing Yip Chinese Restaurant. The dead give-away clue is the claret and blue colours of the gasworks in the distance... This is, after all, the district of Aston, home of Aston Villa FC.

➡ This mini-roundabout is situated on the Selsdon Road, Croydon. By the state of the paintwork on this little chap, drivers have totally ignored the fact that there's an island to be driven around here.

➡ Nunns Corner Roundabout, Grimsby, in full-bloomed glory. The statue of Grim (the founder of Grimsby) is somewhere in the background.

➡ Naird Roundabout, Telford: a solo fir tree planted on top of a scruffy brick roundabout. Could do with a spruce up.

Rabbit Roundabout in Redditch – funnily enough, the home of scores of rabbits. It's often overlooked that roundabouts can be havens for wildlife. This particular island lies just adjacent to Redditch Crematorium.

➡ Bottledump Roundabout in Milton Keynes – not the prettiest of names, but I think it looks okay. Someone has taken the sign literally.

A NAME FOR THE HOBBY

What do you call people who collect data on roundabouts just for fun..? No, apart from that.

The **UK ROUNDABOUT APPRECIATION SOCIETY** (a group of like-minded people, based in Redditch) have had many a heated debate over a suitable moniker.

A few ideas thrown into the pot were:
- Geek Islanders
- Island Hoppers
- Gyrators
- Bouters
- Get-a-lifers

The only name that everyone more or less could agree on was **ROUNDABOUT SPOTTERS**. A **ROUNDABOUT SPOTTER** must have the same attributes as a trainspotter:
- Dedication
- Patience
- Perseverance
- Enthusiasm
- An eye for detail
- Anorak and flask

Only a serious **ROUNDABOUT SPOTTER** understands the particular thrill, the buzz, the rush, the sudden joy of a lush, green oasis on tarmac.

The **UK ROUNDABOUT APPRECIATION SOCIETY** receives many a lead or tip-off on certain locations of exciting traffic-islands, which is great... But you just can't beat those moments when you stumble upon an unexpected island paradise.

➡ A cracking aerial photograph of the Brunel Roundabout in Slough town centre. This traffic-island is also featured in the opening credits of the hit comedy series "The Office". Park-like in its size and appearance – a most attractive roundabout.

➡ An interesting juxtaposition going on here at Skelmersdale Shopping Centre. A hi-tech construction of steel and glass in the background strains against a lacklustre, low-tech mini-roundabout in the foreground.

➡️ An intriguing cone-shaped brick roundabout, which for some reason has a drain attached to it, found on a popular Greater Manchester retail park.

➡ This is a superb example of a brick-built double-ringer island with a great plant arrangement, found on Longmere Road, Solihull. Although the directional bollards are somewhat tilted they do not detract from the overall effect.

➔ Pleasantly undulating, grassy slopes; bushes and trees with autumn leaves; clear direction signs, with CCTV camera. It all adds up to an aesthetically pleasing but functional roundabout. Located on Saxon Drive, Tamworth.

A BRITISH LOVE AFFAIR

Over the past two years, having borne the brunt of every insult and jibe imaginable over my passion for roundabouts, I have to say, hand on heart, that by and large the British love traffic-islands.

But why? My own theory on the subject is that it combines our love of gardens and the fact that we are an island race...

From the numerous letters I receive, all expounding correspondents' fascination with roundabouts, it's not hard to understand what turns them on... The well-manicured lawns, the array of colourful and fragrant flowers, the trees and shrubs, the occasional folly, the wildlife... These horticultural havens provide an uplifting experience on long drab car journeys.

How can anybody not like them? If you could see them through my eyes you wouldn't wonder at all.

➡ What an utterly thrilling experience to witness the birth of an island. One wonders what life will have in store for this fledgling roundabout.

➡ The spindly-looking tree at the centre of this bushy roundabout looks somewhat out of place. However, it's still a good combination of brickwork and foliage. The church in the background sets the scene for a perfect British island.

➡ Set on the fringes of Ilfracombe's town centre, this is a fine level brickwork roundabout, which could be classed as a midi- rather than a mini-roundabout. With its three painted directional arrows, the island covers a surprising area.

 Gypsy Lane Roundabout in the district of Murdoch,
Swindon. Terrific combination of foliage and crazy-paving.
The compost heap to the left looks magnificent.

➡ A rather fetching combination of brickwork, grass and road signs spotted on Claude Road, Barry. The whole effect is somewhat spoilt by the graffiti and the lines of paint crossing the road and island.

➡ Over recent years, this whole island has had a complete makeover. What once could only be described as a bushy jungle now resembles an arid desert. On closer inspection you can make out the odd cactus plant and spiky tropical plant. The road off this roundabout leads to Evesham, home to hundreds of fruit farms.

WHO INVENTED THE ROUNDABOUT?

It would be nice to believe that the British were the first to invent the traffic-island – after all, Stonehenge looks like a roundabout – but, alas, no. Our research shows that the Americans and the French got there first...

According to "Modern Roundabout Practice in the United States" (2003)[1], William Phelps Eno was the bright spark who first devised the idea of a one-way rotary system in 1903, for Columbus Circle, New York City. Other circular traffic systems had existed in the States prior to its implementation in 1904, but these features were primarily architectural and allowed two-way as opposed to one-way traffic circulation. In terms of looks, Eno's roundabouts often consisted of little more than an iron disc of 1.5m (5ft) in diameter, with reflectors or electric lights running around the circumference.

Meanwhile, in France, Eugene Henard – Chief Architect of Paris – had proposed a one-way circulatory system around a central island, which he called a *carrefour à gyration.* Precise dates for this event vary widely between 1877 and 1906, but by 1907, *Place de l'Etoile* (latterly *Place Charles de Gaulle*) was the first French gyratory system in existence. In contrast to Eno's design, Henard's system employed a larger island – a minimum of 8m (26ft) in diameter.

As with most inventions, a passionate debate ensued as to which of these two visionaries came up with the original idea. It is possible that both devised the system independently, but the truth will probably never be known.

[1] "Modern Roundabout Practice in the United States" (2003) National Cooperative Highway Research Program (NCHRP) Synthesis 264, Transportation Research Board, National Research Council/Georges Jacquemart, P.E., AICP, Buckhurst, Fish & Jacquemart, Inc.

➡ A somewhat curious roundabout in close proximity to
De Montfort University, Milton Keynes... Who are those guys?

➡ This little beauty soaks up a few rays not too far from Cleethorpes seafront.

➡ It is fitting that the Bolton Coronary Care Appeal Charity chose a roundabout to display its cause, a roundabout being the heart that pumps the traffic around town and city arteries.

➡ Lombard Roundabout clearly demonstrates how a well-designed island can keep the traffic flowing better than traffic lights. Its other claim to fame is that it featured in the television series "Learner Drivers". Apparently a high percentage of those featured drivers met their Waterloo here.

➡ What a terrific traffic-island this is – spotted in Ironbridge, home of the world's first iron bridge and a town heralding the dawn of the Industrial Revolution. A great juxtaposition of nature and industry encapsulated on one small island – beautiful brickwork, wonderful wrought ironwork, all crowned with a towering tree. It just does not get any better than this.

GREAT BRITAIN AND ON...

While Great Britain cannot claim to have been the place where the roundabout phenomenon started, it was here, according to "Modern Roundabout Practice in the United States", that the term "roundabout" was officially adopted in 1926 to replace the term "gyratory".

Roundabouts have been in operation here since the 1920s – the first being in Letchworth – and since the 1970s, the idea of the traffic-island system has been exported to a number of countries, beginning with Australia, Europe and more recently New Zealand and South Africa.

Ironically, one place the roundabout is not popular in is the USA – the country of its birth.

➡ Sollershott Circus, Letchworth: Britain's first traffic roundabout. Although it was opened to traffic in 1909, it did not become a true "gyratory flow" system until the late 1920s. This roundabout should have a plaque or monument on it declaring its importance.

➡ Anne Hathaway's historic mini-roundabout on the outskirts of Stratford-upon-Avon. Millions of overseas visitors navigate their way around this famous painted island.

➡ Look closely and you'll notice that this mini-roundabout from Barnstable is equipped with a ring of cat's-eyes around its perimeter. Is this the only one in the UK?

➡ This roundabout is fairly new to the Redditch network. It is difficult to see from this shot, but the whole of the island has an undulating surface, prompting local wags to nickname it "The Wobbly Woundabout of Wedditch".

➡ A strange elongated triple-ringer roundabout with a white halo encircling a light red area with a raised inner core. Quite remarkable. Seek this one out in Swansea.

Birmingham A435

Evesham A435

Alcester 4

Abbots Lea
New Homes

FLOWER SHOW & OPEN DAY

➡ This extremely well-kept island with beautiful flowers and interesting dome-shaped brickwork can be found in Studley, England's largest village. Incidentally, the building in the background is not a house but a public convenience.

THE TALE OF TELFORD'S ISLANDS

If you are looking for an exceptional day out roundabout spotting, look no further than Telford. Since 1993, the number of traffic-islands in the new town has more than trebled. It's not purely the quantity of roundabouts that marks Telford out, but the fact that almost every one of its islands boasts some kind of architectural oddity or quality design feature.

However, if the infamous story is to be believed, the origin of Telford's roundabouts owes much more to luck than judgement...

In the mid-1960s, 20 town-planners sat down with a map of the area to decide on the road layout. When they had finished their heated discussions, they picked up their coffee mugs and discovered that each one had left a ring on the map. These 20 rings became Telford's first traffic-islands.

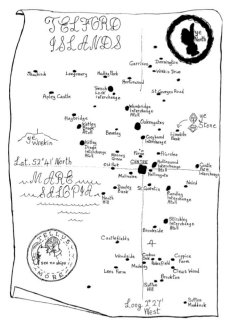

➡ Telford has more islands than a Caribbean treasure map.

➡ Wow! This Telford roundabout is a work of art. Move over Tracy Emin. I'm serious here... If this display was in the Tate Modern it would be worth thousands of pounds. Because it is located on a Telford retail park it is not.

➡ This stunning aerial shot pictures Yellow Pages Roundabout in its full spring glory. Its location is the Town Centre Inner Ring Road, Slough. The only minus factor here is that one or two of the directional signs are in a state of disrepair.

➡ Mermaid Quay... What a lovely name for an island. And doesn't it live up to its name? Great, sloping chevron brickwork is topped off with a beautiful array of plants, trees and rockery. Ten out of ten for Cardiff Council.

➡ Trinity Retail Park Roundabout, Bolton. Cast your eyes to the right of the island and you will see evidence of a slight collision. The yellow grit bin has a hole in it, while the metal bollard protecting the bin has been bent at an alarming angle.

➡ Uniquely, Meads Roundabout on the outskirts of Swindon provides a base for an electricity pylon, proving the point that a traffic-island can accommodate almost anything in its design.

WHAT MAKES A GOOD ROUNDABOUT?

Appreciation of a roundabout is down to personal taste. What appeals to some spotters might not appeal to others, but the whole beauty of roundabout spotting is the infinite variety available... Don't let anyone say it's a boring hobby.

• **Functionality**

First and foremost, a roundabout should do its job. Swindon and Hemel Hempstead's magic roundabouts are not the best-looking traffic-island systems but they both work a treat. Some spotters hate having traffic in their pictures – obviously non-functionalists.

• **Planning**

If you think about it, a lot of planning goes into a roundabout – from the architecture to the horticultural craftwork. The best of the bunch have a touch of genius.

• **Looks**

Some spotters like trees and shrubs, others prefer cropped lawns and gravel. Many islands now have the added attraction of wildlife. Protected from predators by the traffic encircling them, flora and fauna are free to flourish in their roundabout paradise.

• **Character**

Some, like myself, seek that little extra in a roundabout – the quirky features that set an island apart from its brothers and sisters. The roundabout outside Birmingham's Jaguar car plant, for example, has three soaring Spitfires – a tribute to the local production of the aircraft in WW2.

• **Location, Location, Location**

A good backdrop can lift the dullest of mini-islands and can provide an interesting juxtaposition. For example, Windsor Castle has a terrific brick mini-roundabout and Anne Hathaway's cottage in Stratford-upon-Avon boasts a striking painted mini.

➡ This is an all-time favourite. Although there's not a hint of foliage and the whole roundabout has been built and designed on functional grounds, it still has a certain *je ne sais quoi* with its outer-red-ringer and sloping-chevron brickwork capped with a unique tarmac surface and four directional signs. It sits happily in the ASDA supermarket car park in Skelmersdale.

➡ This fine little roundabout can be found behind Brewsters Pub in Grimsby. Note the boulder hiding behind the sign.

➡️ A splendid aerial shot of a busy roundabout in Newport's town centre. The subways on this island are brought to life by tiles depicting rivetting railway scenes.

➡ Midpoint Roundabout logically situated in the Midlands.
It features a strange upside-down pyramid and fine shrubs,
while the protruding brickwork on the outer perimeter sets
it apart from the rest of the pack.

➡ The exciting story behind this little beauty of a mini-roundabout is that it had just received a fresh coat of paint minutes before this picture was taken. Sometimes when you are roundabout spotting you need that extra stroke of luck.

MINI MALPRACTICE

The only problem with painted mini-islands is the careless motorists who keep driving over the poor blighters. Can anybody (apart from me and my fellow UK Roundabout Appreciation Society members) hold their hands up and honestly say, "I have never driven over a painted mini-roundabout."

Those roundabouts were put there for a purpose. We should all observe and navigate accordingly. There's no sight sadder for our society than a downtrodden mini-island criss-crossed with tyre marks.

I don't want to do a soap-box rant here but myself and fellow roundabout spotters are unanimous in believing motorists should never, ever *deliberately* drive over painted minis.

I mean, what's the point in having an island there in the first place if people don't recognise its function and purpose?

The UK Roundabout Appreciation Society members have arrived at the conclusion that there should be a penalty charge of £100 minimum for anyone found guilty of **Mini Malpractice**, coupled with a hefty points penalty on his or her driving licence.

This is something you don't see every day – a mini-red-ringer roundabout with a white painted inner-circle, plus an additional thin white circle with three directional arrows. What a shame that this motorist doesn't seem to recognise its obvious beauty.

➡ A bird's-eye view of a strangely deserted Dingwall Road Roundabout – further proof that roundabouts in London are the way forward to avoid congestion.

➡ A tropical island in Tamworth. A lot of imagination has gone into this little beauty. There are spiky tropical plants, rockery firs and gravel – an oasis on tarmac.

➡️ A painted mini-roundabout with Barry Islands' Log Flume amusement ride in the background.

➡️ Roundabouts are never just thrown together. The designer of this island has added some curious ball-shaped bushes planted equidistantly. The roundabout is a divine combination of brick, gravel and soil, with a tree stuck in the middle.

➡️ This remarkable double-ringer roundabout in South Devon doubles as a bus-stop and a traffic-island. The tree trunk on its raised inner core has faces and seats carved into it.

TYPES OF ROUNDABOUT SPOTTER

Roundabout spotters encompass a very broad church. There are people from all walks of life in our ranks.

On the whole, roundabout spotters are a pretty easy-going and egalitarian bunch. However, over a period of time you notice that there are certain types who hang around the fringes of roundabout circles. This is not intended as a warning but purely guidance.

I've listed a few types below:

The Roundabout Scholar

- Knows the complete history of every roundabout in the area.
- Can also give you leads on traffic-islands in Barrow-in-Furness and Canada.
- Knows the vital statistics of all the mini-roundabouts.
- Always carries a map and compass.
- Has reams of roundabout information on his person amassed from local libraries, town halls and other scholars and technocrat traffic-island inspectors.
- Generally single and male.
- Usually sports a check jacket with leather elbow patches and smokes a pipe.
- Very useful to glean roundabout facts from but never agree to meet later for a drink.

The Technocrat Traffic-Island Inspector

- He lives up to his name: he's not a "spotter"; he *inspects* his islands.
- Can easily be mistaken for the *Roundabout Scholar.*
- Usually the source of a hefty chunk of the *Roundabout Scholar*'s traffic-island knowledge. (This information is always specific to the locality, due to the fact that he never gets out of his own county, as he is too busy measuring and recording statistical data on every roundabout in town.)

- A big gadget man – never to be seen without his Swiss Army knife and electronic tape measure, he also wears a pedometer strapped to his leg to measure the distance between islands.
- Does not take written notes. Instead, he talks into a dictaphone.
- Has been known to do sound recordings of roundabout traffic.
- The only roundabout enthusiast who will go for a drink later with the *Roundabout Scholar.*

The Macho-Type

- Closely related to the sporty-type.
- Wears shorts all year round.
- Walks (but never runs) across the road to the island, even through heavy traffic, sometimes sticking one or even two fingers up at oncoming vehicles.
- Can be found in the middle of the night on a dark, lonely, tree-filled roundabout, laughing to himself whilst taking notes.
- Never argue with him about who has got the best roundabout collection.

The Sporty-Type

- Closely related to the *Macho-Type.*
- Wears £200 trainers and a Nike tracksuit.
- Insists on jogging to all the roundabouts.
- Takes notes without even breaking stride.
- The only spotter who carries a stopwatch.
- Often known to take performance-enhancing substances to achieve a maximum number of roundabouts in one day.

The Pretender

- Tends to be a loner.
- Claims to have seen all the best islands in the world, however, more likely to have never left the county.
- Wears a cagoule rammed with badges of places that he's never been to.
- When showing him your best roundabout pictures he will sneer and try to trump them with his far superior "mega" roundabout collection, which for some reason he can't quite put his hands on.
- Can be a bit of a pain.
- If one does turn up on your committee, the best advice is to boot him off.

➡ A very slightly raised mini-roundabout, which features excellent brickwork. This little character lives somewhere just outside Windsor Castle.

➡ A beautiful roundabout in Swansea town centre, which features a number of trees sprouting proudly from its centre and perimeter... Verdant is the word.

➡ Another Stratford-upon-Avon "Britain in Bloom" winner. The contrast between the black and white chevron brickwork and the explosion of colourful flowers is a sight to behold during the summer months. However, this photograph was taken in mid-October.

➡ This roundabout incorporates an original mine-wheel. The picture was taken on a glorious autumn day in Ironbridge.

➡ This picture of a mini-roundabout in front of Cleethorpes Winter Gardens (currently under threat of closure) has a real "British seaside" feel to it.

➡ An interesting mini-roundabout with a bull's-eye effect, sitting happily outside Swindon Bus Station. Quite hypnotic.

EQUIPMENT TIPS

To become a competent roundabout spotter you must acquire certain essential items, and record key facts and figures.

Notebook & Pen

- Record details such as exits, road names and/or road numbers.
- Take note of any special or unusual features and structures/buildings.
- Work your way from the outer perimeter to the inner core in a methodical manner.
- Swap your material with fellow spotters.
- Ask passers-by if there is any history attached to your discovered roundabout.
- Never trust your own memory – some roundabouts do look alike.
- Always carry a spare pen. You never know.

Camera

- It doesn't need to be expensive – you only need a photograph as a reference aid.
- Do not rely on one picture per island – this could prove disastrous.
- Consider a digital camera – they are perfect for getting your picture just right on the day, but are not as good when it comes to night photography.
- For aerial shots, see if you can spot a choice observation post, such as a multi-storey car park or a block of flats.
- Carry a dirt cheap disposable camera as a back-up...

Tape Measure

- When measuring mini-roundabouts, take two fellow spotters with you – the first to hold the other end of the tape, the second to watch for oncoming traffic.
- If you can't find any fellow spotters, simply pace out the distance, count the steps and measure the length of your own stride. Now use the following formula:

length = number of steps x length of stride

➡ A delightful roundabout just outside Cardiff's city centre, incorporating two fine trees and grass. Captured on a watery but sunny spring day.

➡ A stunning Victorian traffic-island situated on Ilfracombe seafront. Its magnificently ornate wrought-ironwork and beautiful glass globes are complemented by an architecturally interesting backdrop.

➡ Here's a very neat little mini-roundabout in a quiet Studley cul-de-sac. Note the steel barrier protecting this fine island-and-lamp-post partnership from the scourge of reversing cars.

➡️ There is a lot going on in this picture of a Greater Manchester traffic-island. For a start, it's a strange shape. There is a car parked where I suspect it should not be. The location of the island also acts as a bus terminus. The roundabout houses a telephone connection box. In the background a horseless wagon is parked.

➡ A beautiful Bridgnorth roundabout that actually features a bridge (look closely).

TRANSPORT

By Foot

Why not walk between roundabouts? Obviously it's slower and you will not see as many roundabouts as a motorist could, but at least it keeps you fit and you will meet more people on your walks.

Take a road map and work out your route in advance, rather than walking about aimlessly for miles – that would be tiring and non-productive.

By Bike

Due to the fact that you can travel light when roundabout spotting, bicycles are the ideal form of transport: cheap, ecologically sound, and good exercise. And, if you roundabout spot with your wife, you could get a tandem.

But do take care... Roundabouts can be nerve-racking, dangerous places for cyclists. Also, beware of bicycle thieves, particularly when you are examining an especially interesting island.

By Motorbike

For a faster and more convenient form of transport why not go for a motorbike and sidecar? While you concentrate on your driving, your friend or partner can keep their eyes peeled.

By Car

Apart from the obvious comfort factor, the advantage of a car is that you can pack lots of tools and equipment to make your task far easier – e.g. thermos flask, packed lunch, camera, tripod, duffle coat, mittens, etc.

By Mini-Bus

Using a car for lengthy trips can prove extremely expensive. Why not pool your resources with others and hire a mini-bus? There can be no better way of spending a lovely summer's day than driving around a town or city with fellow spotters, savouring the unique delights of the Great British roundabout.

➡ Bramley Hill Roundabout adjacent to Oban House Nursing Home. A fetching combination of silver birch trees, flowers and sloping brickwork.

➡ St Bernard's Road Roundabout, Solihull. An immaculate raised brickwork roundabout with its autumn flowers in full glory... Who said romance was dead?

➡️ Another potentially unique example – this one situated at Newport Hospital – featuring a bold zebra-crossing design, which cuts straight through the island.

➡ The KFC Redditch Red-Ringer... Sounds like an ailment.

➡️ You need to look closely at this picture of a Skelmersdale mini-roundabout to make out that it is a brickwork island and not just a painted mini-roundabout. Also note the bloke running away from the shopping centre.

SAFETY FIRST

Roundabout spotting tends to have a serene image, but any pastime involving road traffic has its dangers.

- Never drive around a roundabout with your head hanging out of the car window, ogling an interesting island.
- Never take photographs while driving your car.
- When a truly stunning roundabout suddenly presents itself in front of you, try to stay in control. I fully understand how hard it is not to get excited but just calm yourself down, pull over to a safe part of the road, take a few deep breaths then inspect your island.
- If you are young or female and the roundabout is on the larger size, with a number of trees and bushes, take a friend and/or a mobile phone.

- Always wear the right clothes: bright ones for visibility; long trousers for protection against nettles and insect bites; lots of layers when the weather is cold; and stout boots – it's amazing what objects you might tread on, the public dump some strange things on roundabouts.
- Watch for burn-out. At first a lot of roundabout spotters try to overdo things, for example attempting too many islands in too many towns in too short a time: 12 roundabouts per day in one town is ample.
- When crossing the road ensure you look left and right.
- Don't go roundabout spotting in Greece. They don't understand the concept yet.

➡ Who said roundabouts are boring? This majestic island in Birmingham boasts three soaring Spitfires in commemoration of the part the aeroplanes played in the Battle of Britain. Just across the road is the Jaguar Assembly Plant, the site where 11,000 of them were manufactured during WW2.

➡ A pretty red-ringer roundabout found in Grasmere, Slough. The reason why the front kerbstones are slanted down to the road is a bit of a mystery.

➡ Which came first: the oak tree or the roundabout? Surely this beauty, located in a quiet Lincolnshire housing estate, is quite unique.

➡ Telford's striking Naird Island with its incredible pyramid.

➡ In the middle of this peaceful island on Oakland Avenue, Barnstable, stands a strange, crucifix-like structure, which doubles as a lamp-post and telegraph pole. Quite intriguing.

➡ Why roundabouts? Surely this picture encapsulates all that's good about the British traffic-island. Observed on a golden October day, the scene depicts two roundabout gardeners taking tender loving care of their Tamworth beauty. The manicured lawn with gorgeous hedges and trees and great angled brickwork make for a perfect roundabout... Superb.

➡ Swindon's Magic Roundabout... What can you say about this one apart from, "Magic!". A true feat of engineering – the traffic is going in the opposite direction to the norm, but the system really works. It has five satellite, conventional roundabouts, all painted in the quirky Swindon bull's-eye effect.

TERRIFIC TRAFFIC-ISLANDS TO COLLECT

Just as a little appetizer to start off your collection, here are my 12 favourite British roundabouts.

• **The Red-Ringer Roundabout, Redditch.** Although it sounds like something nasty, it is in fact a fine example – a *double* red-ringer, no less. You will find it a short stumble away from the KFC Restaurant.

• **The Magic Roundabout, Swindon.** A real feat of engineering, this one (*see opposite*). It comprises one large island and five satellite mini-roundabouts. As you approach the roundabout system at one of the mini-roundabouts, all the traffic comes at you in the wrong direction... Wicked! Located adjacent to Swindon Town FC.

• **The Langley Millennium Roundabout, Slough.** This one celebrates the beginning of a new century – for a really small roundabout it has got so much going for it. Check it out yourself and you will see what I mean.

• **Spitfire Island, Birmingham.** Seek its three spectacular soaring planes outside the Jaguar car plant.

• **The Egg Islands, Tamworth.** You simply can't beat them.

• **The Roundabouts of Skelmersdale.** About 99% of this town's roundabouts are all marvellous – truly a great day out... But don't forget to lock your car.

• **Headless Cross Mini-Roundabout, Worcestershire.** This is in fact the very first mini-roundabout to be used in the UK, and the one featured on "So Graham Norton".

• **The Big W Mini-Roundabout, Bolton.** To be found on Woolworth's retail park. It has a very unusual cone shape.

- **Nunn's Corner Roundabout, Grimsby.** Caught when in full bloom this island dazzles the eye. Presided over by the statue of Grim, the town's founder.

- **Milton Keynes's Entire System.** Another great day out for the roundabout spotter. Your task is made particularly easy by the town's grid system. The perfect place to get started in your new hobby.

- **The Roundabouts of Solihull and Stratford-Upon-Avon.** These two towns are perennial contenders for the "Britain in bloom" crown. Catch their roundabouts at the right time and you will be in horticultural heaven.

- **The Mini-Island, Windsor Castle.** Modest in size, but nonetheless a lovely brick-built mini, possessing a spectacular backdrop.

➡ A smart painted mini-roundabout on the South Wales coast – a beacon of white on an overcast day.

⮕ A double-ringer roundabout on the Enfield Industrial Estate on the twelfth day of Christmas.

➡ Racecourse Roundabout, Stratford-upon-Avon. The island consists of an outer perimeter of brickwork, shrub, trees and soil. The picture was taken on a Sunday – a non-race day.

➡ A lush traffic-island adjacent to Jaipur's Curry Palace, Milton Keynes. Those amazing round trees set on tiered lawns with the colonial style building in the background give this roundabout a truly exotic look.

➡ You could almost term this island located on a quiet Shirley street a triple-ringer. On close inspection there are three different types of brickwork, capped off with raised kerb stone and even more fine brickwork and bollard.

➡ This somewhat serene-looking island resides on Bolton's Whitecroft Road. It is triangular in shape with a waste-paper bin, four 'No Parking' signs and a bench seat for weary travellers to rest for a while.

➡️ A historic first for Worcestershire... This roundabout at Headless Cross was the very first mini-traffic-island to be used in the UK. A great success story.

➡ An interesting example of a traffic-island set inside a peaceful undertaker's car park.

Acknowledgements

Special thanks must go to Jason Holmes and Lee Beresford for keeping my company going whilst Liz Austin (photographer) and myself were combing the country looking for choice roundabouts; The Transportation Research Board, National Research Council in the US, for providing important information on the history of roundabouts in "Modern Roundabout Practice in the United States"; and Colin Purkis for information on Telford's roundabout system.

I'd also like to mention my late father, Harry, who worked on Birmingham's road system all his life. My love for roundabouts must surely be in the genes.

The UK Roundabout Appreciation Society is a group of like-minded people who meet on a regular basis swapping photographs and data on all types of roundabouts. They are based in Redditch and can be contacted via website www.roundaboutsofbritain.com or by email on kevin@beresfordb96.freeserve.co.uk. The current members are:

Liz Austin	Dan Fritzgerald	Simon Mawdsley
B. Bailey	Deb Fritzgerald	Phil McInerny
Elliot Beresford	Clive Gallimore	Pat McManus
Kevin Beresford	Norma Gray	Shirley Murkin
Lee Beresford	Sally Green	Chris O'Riordan
Linda Beresford	Sue Hamlyn	Joan Pratten
Bev Burchell	Phil Handford	Roger Spence
Jo Carter	Ernie Hill	Brian Summers
Dave Clark	Jason Holmes	Wally Tynan
Paul Clarke	Heather Honeypot	Jon Williamson
Richard Coffin	Helen Johnson	Tony Wilson
Ray Davis	Howard Jones	

Dedicated to my long-suffering wife.
I will always be there for you
if you decide to come back.

First published in 2004 by
New Holland Publishers (UK) Ltd
London • Cape Town • Sydney • Auckland
www.newhollandpublishers.com

Garfield House
86–88 Edgware Road
London W2 2EA
United Kingdom

80 McKenzie Street
Cape Town 8001
South Africa

14 Aquatic Drive
Frenchs Forest
NSW 2086
Australia

218 Lake Road
Northcote
Auckland
New Zealand

10 9 8 7 6 5 4 3 2

Editor: Gareth Jones
Editorial Direction: Rosemary Wilkinson
Production: Hazel Kirkman
Designer: Bill Mason
Photographer: Liz Austin
Night Photographer: Ray Davis
Map (p38): Telford & Wrekin Council

Reproduction by Modern Age Repro, Hong Kong
Printed and bound by Craft Print International,
Singapore

➡ Is this a roundabout? I believe so. It's certainly an island...
It has directional signs on it... It has traffic going around it...
It's a roundabout in my book. This lovely brick and wrought
iron piece is situated not far from Gas Street Basin in
Birmingham, the hub of Britain's canal system. The picture was
taken from the balcony of the Malt Shovel Public House, where
President Clinton enjoyed a pint of ale and a bag of fish and
chips whilst attending the G8 World Summit Meeting.